MY
PRAYER
LANGUAGE

A Guide to Spirit-Empowered Prayer

STEPHANIE TRAYERS

ISBN: 9798642689325

Eddie Trayers
Lead Pastor, Summit Church
Springfield, Virginia

CONTENTS

INTRODUCTION

When we receive Christ, we begin a journey with Him that transforms our lives! Forgiveness of our sins, peace with God, and an assurance of eternity with Him are some of the great blessings of our new life in Jesus. On this new spiritual journey, we have the opportunity to receive another blessing—the gift of the Holy Spirit. Jesus described the Holy Spirit as a Helper and One who would empower us as we live for God (see Acts 1:8; John 14:16).

Jesus promised His followers that they would receive the baptism of the Holy Spirit.

> On one occasion, while he [Jesus] was eating with them [the disciples], he gave them this command: "Do not leave Jerusalem, but wait for the gift my Father promised, which you have heard me speak about. For John baptized with water, but in a few days you will be baptized with the Holy Spirit." (Acts 1:4–5 NIV, bracketed text added)

He also told His followers that one of the signs that would follow those who believe in Him would be the ability to *"speak with new languages."*

He who believes and is baptized will be saved; but he who disbelieves will be condemned. These signs will accompany those who believe: in my name they will cast out demons; <u>they will speak with new languages;</u> they will take up serpents; and if they drink any deadly thing, it will in no way hurt them; they will lay hands on the sick, and they will recover. (Mark 16:16–18 WEB, emphasis added)

Soon after Jesus ascended into Heaven, His promise came to pass. And with this baptism came the ability to speak in different languages.

When the day of Pentecost came, they were all together in one place. Suddenly a noise came from heaven. It sounded like a strong wind blowing. This noise filled the whole house where they were sitting. They saw something that looked like flames of fire. The flames were separated and stood over each person there. <u>They were all filled with the Holy Spirit, and they began to speak different languages. The Holy Spirit was giving them the power to do this</u>. (Acts 2:1–4 ERV, emphasis added)

Jesus told the disciples to wait for the promise of the Holy Spirit, but they had no idea what to expect. They did not ask for new languages or seek to receive prayer languages. The languages were God's idea. This is important for us to remember because having a new language seems strange to our natural minds. But God said, *"My thoughts and my ways are not like yours. Just as the heavens are higher than the earth, my thoughts and my ways are higher than yours."* (Isaiah 55:8–9 CEV)

Speaking in other languages may sound strange to us, but it is not strange that God would use languages to serve His purposes. God used language to create the world (see Genesis 1:1–31; Hebrews 11:3). He separated human beings from all His other creations by giving language to Adam and Eve. Through spoken language, we communicate with God and one another. Through written language, we learn about God, His Son Jesus, and His plan for our salvation. To receive this salvation, we believe in our heart and use our mouth (language) to confess Him as our Savior (see Romans 10:9–10). In this book, we're going to look at various ways God uses Holy Spirit–given languages to serve His purpose of empowering our prayer life.

How to Use This Book

There are many types of prayer and all are beneficial to our walk with Christ, but I will focus solely on praying in our prayer language in this book. *My Prayer Language* consists of 11 short chapters containing a particular truth about Spirit-empowered prayer. You'll see that each chapter references scriptures, which I encourage you to meditate on and study on your own. You can use the questions at the end of each chapter for reflection and small-group discussion.

There is much more to learn about praying in a prayer language than what I have included in this book. I have provided a list of recommended books for further study in the "Additional Resources" section (p. 61). If you are a Christ-follower but have not been filled with the Holy Spirit, may I suggest you begin by reading a book on the subject of Holy Spirit baptism, such as *The Holy Spirit Today*, by John Siebeling, or *The God I Never Knew*, by Robert Morris.

I hope *My Prayer Language* will be an encouraging resource for you, whether you have recently received your prayer language or have been using your prayer language for years.

CHAPTER 1

PRAYING IN THE SPIRIT

If I pray in a different language, my spirit is praying ...
1 Corinthians 14:14 ERV

The first truth we must consider when studying the subject of praying in a prayer language is *whom* we are speaking to. The Word provides a clear perspective: *"For the person who speaks in another language is not speaking to men but to God ..."* (1 Corinthians 14:2 HCSB).

Our prayer language is a direct line of communication to *God.* This is a tremendous truth that we should view with the same awe and honor we strive to give to Him in every other area of worship and prayer.

You may have heard people describe praying in a prayer language as "praying in tongues," "praying in a heavenly language," or—as I'll usually say in this book—"praying in the Spirit." We know we're praying "in the Spirit" when we pray in our prayer language because 1 Corinthians 14:2 continues by saying that the person who speaks in another language *"speaks mysteries <u>in the Spirit</u>"* (HCSB, emphasis added).

Another essential truth to realize about our new heavenly language is that it is a means for our spirit to pray. In other words, it is a way for the part of us that connects with God to speak out.

> **If I pray in a different language, <u>my spirit is praying</u>, but my mind does nothing. So what should I do? I will pray with my spirit, but I will also pray with my mind. ... (1 Corinthians 14:14–15 ERV, emphasis added)**

This verse explains that praying with our mind and praying with our spirit are different. You may have never thought about it this way before, but when we pray in our prayer language, *our spirit prays.* Using our prayer language allows our spirit to express itself like never before.

Jesus gave us a clue that He would give us access to this type of praying in one of His descriptions of the Holy Spirit.

> **The last day of the festival came. It was the most important day. On that day Jesus stood up and said loudly, "Whoever is thirsty may come to me and drink. If anyone believes in me, <u>rivers of living water will flow out from their heart</u>. That is what the Scriptures say."**

Jesus was talking about the Spirit. The Spirit had not yet been given to people, because Jesus had not yet been raised to glory. But later, those who believed in Jesus would receive the Spirit. (John 7:37–39 ERV, emphasis added)

Praying with our spirit, from our heart, occurs when we pray in the language given to us when we received the baptism of the Holy Spirit. Now don't let the word *language* intimidate you. You may have prayed with what sounded like a language when you received this baptism. Or maybe your current prayer "language" sounds nothing like a language. Do not be concerned about that. Instead, remember that the Bible also describes the language of praying in the Spirit as *groaning*.

And the Holy Spirit helps us in our weakness. For example, we don't know what God wants us to pray for. But the Holy Spirit prays for us with <u>groanings that cannot be expressed in words</u>. (Romans 8:26 NLT, emphasis added)

Groaning does not sound like a language, but it is one way to describe praying in the Spirit. You may have experienced what sounds more like groans than a fluent language. The point is, we do not need to dissect the sounds coming from our spirit; we need to believe and understand that it is the Holy Spirit helping us to pray. The more your spirit prays in the language or sounds it has been given, the more fluent your language will become.

Another thing to notice in 1 Corinthians 14:14 is that when we pray with our spirit, our mind *"does nothing."* This is a new experience for us. Our minds have always prayed until now. Our minds will not understand what we are praying in this new language. Your mind may even tell you that you are wasting your time because it is used to understanding what you are talking to God about.

Do not give in to the temptation to quit praying in the Spirit and go back to only praying with your mind. Remember that your spirit has not had a chance to pray like this before. Although it will feel different to have your mind do nothing, know that something great is happening while your spirit prays!

Reflection Questions

1. How does it make you feel to know that the baptism of the Holy Spirit allows your spirit to pray things that your mind can't understand?

2. Have you ever been tempted to stop praying in the Spirit because of the way your language sounds?

3. What will you do to become more fluent in your prayer language?

CHAPTER 2

CHARGING OUR SPIRIT

The person who speaks in another language
<u>builds himself up</u> ...
1 Corinthians 14:4 HCSB, emphasis added

But you, beloved, keep <u>building up yourselves</u> on your
most holy faith, <u>praying in the Holy Spirit</u>.
Jude 1:20 WEB, emphasis added

These verses from 1 Corinthians and Jude tell us that we build ourselves up when we pray in the Spirit. In the last chapter, we learned that our spirit prays when we pray in this new language. Therefore, it is our spirit that is built up every time we pray in the Spirit.

We all know what it's like to have devices that need to be charged. We have become dependent on these devices, especially our phones. We use them all day to conduct business, connect with others, and enjoy entertainment. Because our devices have become such a valuable resource in our daily lives, we have become intentional about keeping these devices charged. As useful as they are to us, they are of no use when they have not been charged—as we have all discovered at one time or another!

In a similar way, praying in the Spirit charges and builds up our spirits. This is one of the many benefits of our prayer language. It's important that we take time to charge our spirits so that we can operate "fully charged." Our phones die when they are not charged. Our spirits will not die, but we will not be empowered to the place of strength God has planned for us to be in if we do not take the time to charge ourselves up.

We need to charge our devices because we use them every day. We need to charge our spirits because we use our faith every day. The Bible says Christians live and walk by faith (see Galatians 3:11; 2 Corinthians 5:7). And notice that Jude 1:20 says we are building ourselves up in our *"most holy faith."* Many times we begin to pray in the Spirit feeling like our faith is weak, but after we have spent time praying, our faith is strengthened and we are ready to use our faith! For example, if we are confused about a situation, we may be strengthened to the place of having peace. If we need direction, we may sense God's leading. If we are discouraged, our faith may be strengthened to believe God's promises are true.

Since praying in the Spirit is so vital to our spiritual edification, it's no wonder that we often feel doubtful, weak, and empty spiritually when we haven't taken the time to do it. We feel as if we are running on empty because we haven't done our part to charge!

It's exciting to think about what happens when we charge our spirits this way. You see, our spirits were born of God and created in Christ. So when we pray in the Spirit, our hearts plug into the One who created us. We are not of this world, so we must plug into the place we are from and where we were created—a place in the spirit realm called *in Christ Jesus*. When we take time to let our spirits charge, we can go back into the natural world equipped with power! (See 1 John 5:4; Ephesians 2:10; John 17:16; Acts 1:8.)

As mentioned in the previous chapter, our minds do nothing when our spirits pray in the Holy Spirit. You are not going to know what you are saying in your prayer language, but that's okay. Just "charge." Your time is never wasted when you disconnect from everything else and plug into the Spirit. You will build yourself up and be empowered to live for Christ!

Reflection Questions

1. Does it feel like your spiritual battery is low right now or fully charged?

2. How would being built up in your faith influence your life?

3. How can you adjust your schedule to make sure you are plugging into the Holy Spirit daily?

CHAPTER 3

PRAYING THE WILL OF GOD

*... the Spirit pleads for us believers in harmony
with God's own will.*
Romans 8:27 NLT

I have never met a Christian who did not want to know what God's will is for him or her. That is probably the greatest desire of any sincere Christian's heart. Knowing that what we are doing and what we are planning to do is part of God's perfect will for us would bring such spiritual peace and satisfaction, wouldn't it? Good news: This chapter will show you how you can have the knowledge you seek by praying in your prayer language.

Knowing that we are praying in agreement with God's will begins with making sure our prayers are filled with the truths and promises that He has already spoken. In other words, we should pray what we have already heard God say in scripture. Here's how Jesus put it:

If you remain in me and <u>my words remain in you</u>, ask for whatever you want and it will be done for you. (John 15:7 CEB, emphasis added)

We also have a promise that if we make requests in prayer that are in line with His will, then God will give us those things we ask for.

This is the confidence that we have in our relationship with God: If we ask for anything in agreement with his will, he listens to us. If we know that he listens to whatever we ask, we know that we have received what we asked from him. (1 John 5:14–15 CEB)

These two scriptures give us great assurance that we will have what we've asked for in prayer. When we base our prayers on His Word, we are praying in agreement with His will. He will hear us and answer us.

But what about the times when we don't know what His will is for us? The times when we don't have scripture for our particular situation? There will be times throughout our lives when we will need to know God's will concerning a relationship, where to go to school, what job to take, where to live, what car or home to buy, when to start a family, and other important decisions.

Thank God the Bible gives us a solution in times like these!

And the Holy Spirit helps us in our weakness. For example, we don't know what God wants us to pray for. But the Holy Spirit prays for us with groanings that cannot be expressed in words. And the Father who knows all hearts knows what the Spirit is saying, for <u>the Spirit pleads for us believers in harmony with God's own will</u>. And we know that God causes everything to work together for the good of those who love God and are called according to his purpose for them. (Romans 8:26–28 NLT, emphasis added)

When we pray in the Spirit, the Spirit helps us in our weakness of not knowing God's will concerning some of life's most important decisions. I have experienced this in my own life.

When I graduated from high school, I struggled with deciding which college I should attend. My hometown option was a college where my dad worked, so I could attend that college tuition-free. My second option was an out-of-state school that I had been considering for a couple of years. Every day for weeks, I would talk to my family and friends about the pros and cons of staying close to home or leaving the state.

I finally met with my pastor about my dilemma, and he gave me some of the greatest spiritual advice I have ever received. He listened to my reasons for staying home and my reasons for going out of state. He then told me to go home and pray in the Spirit. He explained that praying in the Spirit is a spiritual exercise and that we fine-tune our spirits to hear God's voice when we pray this way. He encouraged me to pray for a while, then listen to what my heart was saying and make my decision. He also instructed me not to change my mind once I made my decision.

I left my pastor's office and went straight home and began to pray. Within about 20 minutes, I knew that my mind—my own human reasoning—was telling me to stay home and go to school. But God, speaking to my spirit, was telling me to go to the out-of-state school. This was a step of faith for me financially, but in the following weeks I discovered that my tuition at the out-of-state school would be covered. And one year later, I found out the main reason God led me to this school when I met my future husband!

When we do not know what decision we should make, the Holy Spirit is within us to help us pray the will of the Father. He will help us distinguish what our head is telling us to do from what our heart is telling us to do. Of course, we make many decisions in life with our own mental reasoning. But a big problem with our reasoning is that we do not know what the future holds for us. But God, who lives in our spirits, knows our future, so we can trust His leading in our hearts when we pray.

When you want to find out God's will regarding a decision you are facing, start by telling God your dilemma (see Proverbs 3:5–6). Then begin to pray in the Spirit, in your prayer language. Remember that Romans 8 tells us the Holy Spirit prays for us *"in harmony with God's own will."*

It may take a day or two (maybe a little longer) of intentionally praying in the Spirit about your decision, but stay with it until you receive a sense of peace about the decision you should make.

> And <u>let the peace</u> (soul harmony which comes) from Christ <u>rule</u> (act as umpire continually) in your hearts <u>[deciding and settling with finality all questions that arise in your minds</u>, in that peaceful state] to which as [members of Christ's] one body you were also called [to live]. And be thankful (appreciative), [giving praise to God always]. (Colossians 3:15 AMPC, emphasis added)

Once you make your decision based on the peace in your heart, do not change your mind. Understand and value the fact that God has led you to this decision, and trust that He knows the future better than you do.

God wants to lead you into His will for your life and now, with the help of the Holy Spirit, you can pray in perfect agreement with His will.

Reflection Questions

1. Have you ever had a decision to make but struggled between your own human reasoning and what your heart was saying?

2. Has there been a time when you sought out God's will and followed it? What were the results?

3. Do you have an important decision to make right now? Try using the strategies outlined in this chapter to pursue God's will on the matter.

CHAPTER 4

SPEAKING MYSTERIES

For the person who speaks in another language is not speaking to men but to God, since no one understands him; however, he speaks mysteries in the Spirit.

1 Corinthians 14:2 HCSB

This verse tells us an amazing truth that's worth paying close attention to. When we are praying in our prayer language, we are praying *to God,* and *no one*—not even our spiritual enemy—can understand these secrets we are praying to our Heavenly Father. Note that there are different kinds of languages in the Spirit. Some languages we may speak in the Spirit are languages on earth, but a language the speaker does not understand. (See 1 Corinthians 12:28, 13:1; Acts 2:1-11.) However, our focus scripture refers to a language in the Spirit that is not a language on earth.

We speak mysteries in the Spirit when we pray in our prayer language. What is the purpose of that? Well, have you ever read a mystery novel or watched a mystery on TV? The plot builds until the mystery is finally solved. We are eager to hear the end of the story when the detective fills us in on how he solved the mystery. The whole point of the story is to understand the mystery in the end and for the truth to be *revealed*.

When we pray in our prayer language, we are praying about things that are still mysteries to us but not mysteries to God. The Holy Spirit causes these "mystery prayers" to come out of our spirits and up to God. They may have to do with our own lives or the life of someone we care for. When the time is right, God will reveal the mystery. He will give us or the person we prayed for the revelation needed for that particular situation.

I want to remind you of a passage we looked at in the introduction.

He who believes and is baptized will be saved; but he who disbelieves will be condemned. These signs will accompany those who believe: in my name they will cast out demons; <u>they will speak with new languages</u>; they will take up serpents; and if they drink any deadly thing, it will in no way hurt them; they will lay hands

on the sick, and they will recover. (Mark 16:16-18 WEB, emphasis added)

Each sign that Jesus said will accompany believers is supernatural, including speaking in new languages. You may be familiar with the idea of God answering prayer through circumstances or by bringing a scripture to your mind, but the idea of God speaking to an individual or of a person seeing a vision may be new to you. When we pray in our prayer language, we are praying in a deeper dimension. At times, this will bring about answers that are just as supernatural as the prayer language itself. (See Acts 2:17, 8:26-35, 9:1-18, 10:9-20.)

I would like to share a personal example of how God answered one of my prayers in the Spirit. When the time came for my youngest daughter to begin school, she missed the age deadline by three days. I was disappointed that she would be four school years apart from her older sister. However, she could attend a private kindergarten, be tested, and then placed in public school for first grade. I had prayed in the Spirit about the situation, but a day came when I told the Lord that I did not want to push for anything that was not right for my daughter and gave the matter to Him. When I did, He spoke to my heart, "Decidedly yes." And immediately, I saw a little vision. I saw glass doors like the automatic ones you find in front of a grocery store. I walked up to the doors expecting them to open when I got to them, but they did not open when I stepped right in front of them, so I had to stop. But as soon as I stopped, they opened and I walked through them. So based on this "revelation," I put my daughter in private kindergarten and followed the steps I had been instructed to do in order to place her in first grade. But after taking those steps, the doors closed. She was placed in kindergarten again. I had to "stop" just like I saw in the vision, but within a few days those doors opened, and she was placed in first grade.

That story shares a revelation I received in prayer that regarded my *natural life*. Paul, who wrote the 1 Corinthians verse about speaking mysteries, is a good example of someone who received revelation concerning his *spiritual life*.

Paul understood the value of speaking in his prayer language. He said he prayed in the Spirit more than all the people in the church he was writing to (see 1 Corinthians 14:18). He had received great revelation from praying in the Spirit. As a matter of fact, Paul said the gospel he preached was given to him by revelation from God, not from any human being (see Galatians 1:11–12). Speaking mysteries brought him a revelation for his particular gifting in life.

There are also biblical truths and revelations that God would like us to receive that will benefit our spiritual life, but we cannot grasp them in our minds, so they remain a mystery.

I grew up in church and knew I was "supposed" to read my Bible, but I did not enjoy reading it. However, when I was a junior in high school, that changed. One Wednesday night in my youth group at church, one of my youth leaders shared an interesting story from a Christian book he was reading. I remembered that my parents had that book at home. The next day, I took the book off our living room bookshelf and brought it to school with me. While sitting in study hall, I read this statement: "Find scriptures that promise you the things you're praying for." For some reason, the lightbulb came on for me when I read that statement.

I decided to do just what the statement said. I dealt with depression as a teenager, so I began to look for scriptures that gave me promises of hope during the time I spent reading my Bible. I would read a chapter or so and write down in a notebook any scriptures that stood out to me. I began to find that many scriptures stood out, not only promises of hope but also verses that challenged me to be a better Christian. Then the next time I would read my Bible, I would also read and meditate on the verses I had collected in my notebook. I did this for several months when one day something amazing happened.

I remember that day because it was the day I experienced victory in my mind for the first time. I was sitting alone in my car at a stoplight when the familiar feeling of depression began to come over me. But this time, something different happened. Those scriptures that I had been meditating on that spoke of the good things God said about me were beginning to drop into my heart. Suddenly this time, when I felt the depression, words came up out of my heart, into my mind, and out of my mouth as I quoted Psalms 23:6 (KJV), *"Surely goodness and mercy shall follow me all the days of my life: and I will dwell in the house of the Lord forever."* Immediately, the feeling of depression left me. I sat there thinking, "Wow, that really worked!"

Being in the ministry for more than 30 years, I have shared that story countless times. And often I have said, as I just shared with you, that it was like a lightbulb came on for me that day. Many years later, the Lord told me that it was my mom's prayers in the Spirit for me that brought me that revelation. Her prayers brought me a spiritual revelation that changed my life.

So you see, praying in our prayer language brings revelation. Revelation for something that may affect our natural life or revelation that may affect our spiritual life.

Revelations that God gives us are not so spiritual that only the most spiritually mature people can understand them. On the contrary, revelation makes the Word of God *easy to understand.* It's like a lightbulb turns on. We see clearer and understand the truth like never before!

Praying mysteries in the Spirit will lead you into revelations that God has planned for you to receive.

Reflection Questions

1. How does knowing that you are praying to God alone and that even your spiritual enemy cannot understand you change your perspective on praying in the Spirit?

2. Has God ever spoken to you when you were praying in your prayer language?

3. What revelation from God are you seeking right now? How can praying in the Spirit help it be revealed?

CHAPTER 5

SEARCHING IN THE SPIRIT

... The Spirit searches all things, even the
deep things of God.

1 Corinthians 2:10 NIV

The Bible teaches us that the Spirit searches the deep things of God. Deep things are not on the surface. My granddaddy was a coal miner in West Virginia. He would come home from work covered in black soot. He had a Volkswagen Beetle that he drove to and from work that was also covered in the soot. Of course, I never rode in that car, my grandmother would not allow it! And she would not allow him in the house after work until he showered in the basement using dishwashing liquid to take off the dirt! Miners get very dirty because they do not work on the surface of the earth. They have to go *deeper*.

That is what is meant by the Scriptures which say that no mere man has ever seen, heard, or even imagined what wonderful things God has ready for those who

love the Lord. But we know about these things because God has sent his Spirit to tell us, and <u>his Spirit searches out and shows us all of God's deepest secrets</u>. No one can really know what anyone else is thinking or what he is really like except that person himself. And <u>no one can know God's thoughts except God's own Spirit</u>. And God has actually given us his Spirit (not the world's spirit) to tell us about the <u>wonderful free gifts of grace and blessing that God has given us</u>. (1 Corinthians 2:9–12 TLB, emphasis added)

God has *"wonderful things"* planned for us that we have never even imagined. The Holy Spirit is able to show us these things. When we give time to praying in our prayer language, we give the Holy Spirit time to search the things that God has ready for us. He even searches the deep secrets of God. Some of the things God has for us, although still a secret, include the following:

- Knowledge—something we need to understand about our natural life or spiritual life

- Wisdom—something we need to do in our natural life or spiritual life

- Victory—His search always leads to victory in our natural life or spiritual life

Colossians 2:3 (CSB) tells us that *"In him are hidden all the treasures of wisdom and knowledge."* There are treasures of wisdom and knowledge still hidden in Jesus. Some of these treasures are the wisdom and knowledge you need for a particular situation in your *natural life.* Maybe you have prayed for years about a situation that needs to change. To find the answer, you will have to go deeper. *You* can't go deeper, but the Holy Spirit can. Just like no one knows what you are thinking except your own spirit, no one knows God's thoughts except His Spirit.

When we pray in our prayer language, the Holy Spirit begins to search the deep things of God—that is, the thoughts of God that pertain to our situation. He is searching for treasure, a treasure of wisdom or a treasure of knowledge hidden in Christ.

Treasures are never on the surface of the earth; they are hidden. If you want to find them, you have to search for them. For us to be able to understand the treasures hidden in Christ for us, we will need to give the Holy Spirit opportunities to search through us in our praying.

Just think, Jesus may have a treasure of wisdom for you that you have never seen before. This could be wisdom He wants you to have when you have done everything and nothing has worked. He may have a treasure of knowledge for you—something you need to understand that will help your situation.

As with any valuable hidden treasure, searching will have to take place. And it takes time to search. It would be to your advantage to give time to pray in your prayer language so that the Holy Spirit can have time to search for the treasures of wisdom and knowledge hidden for you.

What about those deeply hidden secrets and treasures that pertain to our *spiritual life?* The key for us to understand is found in this little phrase from Colossians 2:3, *in Him.* All of the victory God has provided for us is found in Him—that is, "In Christ."

Some of these treasures He has hidden *for* us are in our discovering who we are, what we have, and what we can do "In Christ." For example, God wants us to have knowledge of the fact that before Jesus went to Heaven, He gave the Church authority over any evil that could touch our lives. Then, He wants us to have wisdom concerning that fact— what to *do* with the knowledge that Jesus gave us authority. He wants us to *use* the authority He has given us. (See Matthew 18:18, 28:18–20; James 4:7; Luke 10:19.)

We can read scriptures that tell us these things, but the Holy Spirit searches the deep meaning of truths like these when we pray in our prayer language. He then shows the truths to us in a way that will make them a vital reality in our spiritual lives.

Another benefit of the Holy Spirit searching the deep things of God is His help in prayer when we are deeply hurting, saddened, or burdened about situations in our lives.

Our pain may be deep, but when we begin to pray in our prayer language, the Holy Spirit goes to a deep place in God to find our help. The deep groanings and longings of the Spirit match our deep hurt. After a while, something amazing happens. We begin to sense a deep peace that is just as pronounced as the deep hurt we were feeling earlier in prayer. The Holy Spirit brings us from deep pain to deep prayer to deep peace.

No matter what our need is, the Holy Spirit searches for the victory that is ours in Christ for the situations we are praying about (see 1 Corinthians 15:57). One thing is for sure: His searching *always* leads to our victory!

As we pray in our prayer language, the Holy Spirit will search the deep things of God and pull up treasures that will be great blessings in our lives.

Reflection Questions

1. Take some time to meditate on this thought:

   No one can really know what anyone else is thinking or what he is really like except that person himself. And no one can know God's thoughts except God's own Spirit. And God has actually given us his Spirit (not the world's spirit) to tell us about the wonderful free gifts of grace and blessing that God has given us. (1 Corinthians 2:11–12 TLB)

   What does this truth mean to you? How can understanding this truth impact your prayer life?

2. Are you in need of more wisdom or knowledge right now? What is the difference between the two?

3. Can you think of a time when deep pain led to deep prayer and then deep peace?

CHAPTER 6

PRAYING WITH THE HELPER

And the Holy Spirit helps us in our weakness. ...
Romans 8:26 NLT

To fully appreciate the help of the Holy Spirit, we need to remember who He is. God is a being composed of three equal parts: God the Father, God the Son, and God the Holy Spirit. *God the Holy Spirit* is helping us in prayer, which is the same as saying that *God* is helping us in prayer. That's why the help the Holy Spirit provides is greater than any help a human being can give us.

And the Holy Spirit helps us in our weakness. For example, we don't know what God wants us to pray for. But the Holy Spirit prays for us with groanings that cannot be expressed in words. And the Father who knows all hearts knows what the Spirit is saying, for

the Spirit pleads for us believers in harmony with God's own will. And we know that God causes everything to work together for the good of those who love God and are called according to his purpose for them. (Romans 8:26–28 NLT)

Let's look at some of the ways the Holy Spirit helps us in prayer.

He helps us pray beyond our understanding. This passage from Romans tells us that we have a "weakness" in prayer: *"we don't know what God wants us to pray for."* This is a very interesting thought. We know through numerous scriptures that God hears and answers our prayers. But there must be prayers that "God wants us to pray" that we do not know about, causing a weakness in our prayer time. Thank God that *"the Holy Spirit helps us in our weakness"* as He *"prays for us with groanings that cannot be expressed in words."*

God knows that the prayers we *should* be praying—prayers that we do not know to pray—would bring answers and blessings to our lives and the lives of others. So when we pray in our prayer language, the Holy Spirit helps by praying these unknown prayers through us.

If we knew about the unforeseen challenges and problems we were going to face in our day, we would pray about them. When we pray in the Spirit, that's exactly what we are doing! The Holy Spirit helps us to pray about the things in our life that we do not know to pray about.

He helps us pray for people who have not yet received Christ. John 3:16 tells us that God loved the world so much that He gave His only Son to free us from our sin and gift us with eternal life. He loves every human being on the earth more than we do. One of the advantages to praying in our prayer language is the help the Holy Spirit gives us when we pray for others. Let's look at part of the Holy Spirit's role on earth.

> **Nevertheless I tell you the truth. It is to your advantage that I go away; for if I do not go away, <u>the Helper</u> will not come to you; but If I depart, I will send Him to you. And when He has come, He will <u>convict the world</u> of sin, and of righteousness, and of judgment ... (John 16:7–8 NKJV, emphasis added)**

Our Helper, the Holy Spirit, has come to convict people. We see this conviction at work on the first day believers were filled with the Spirit. On that day, the gospel was preached to thousands of people who *"came under deep conviction and said to Peter and the rest of the apostles: 'Brothers, what must we do?'"* (Acts 2:37 HCSB).

Imagine that! The conviction they experienced through the preaching of the gospel was so strong that no one had to ask them to receive Christ, *they* asked what to do to receive Christ! When we pray in our prayer language for people who do not yet know Christ, the Holy Spirit goes to work inside of those individuals to begin to convict them. He knows how to go deep into their hearts, as we see in these verses, and prepare them to receive the gospel.

He helps us pray for other Christians. God knows what people need more than we do. When we pray in our prayer language for our brothers and sisters in Christ, the Holy Spirit prays God's will for them through us.

And <u>pray in the Spirit</u> on all occasions with all kinds of prayers and requests. <u>With this in mind</u>, be alert and always <u>keep on praying for all the Lord's people</u>. (Ephesians 6:18 NIV, emphasis added)

Without the Holy Spirit's help, it would be impossible to pray *"for all the Lord's people."* But when we are praying in the Spirit, He enables us to pray for the ones He knows need our prayers. While praying in your prayer language, you may at times speak words or names in your natural language. These are words or names that you did not think about or plan to say. You may be surprised when you speak these words in the middle of praying in your prayer language, but just realize that this is the Holy Spirit praying through you about people and situations you do not know about.

He helps us pray for everything to work out. The Word of God shows us different types of prayers we can pray and receive answers for. If we ask for wisdom, we are promised to receive it (see James 1:5). We are instructed not to worry but to pray about our problems, and we are promised to be given peace (see Philippians 4:6–7). We are told to acknowledge God in the various situations of our lives and that He will answer by guiding our paths (see Proverbs 3:5–6). We can ask for certain things and receive corresponding answers (see Matthew 21:22).

Let's take a look at Romans 8 again to see how God answers prayer when we pray with the help of the Holy Spirit.

And we know that God causes everything to work together for the good of those who love God and are called according to his purpose for them. (Romans 8:28 NLT)

The answer to Spirit-led praying is everything working together for good. As you make praying in your prayer language a consistent part of your spiritual life, you will discover that God works things out for you and works in those situations you have in your heart. *Everything working together for our good* is an answer to prayer that we often overlook. We may not always realize that things are working out for our good because the "working out" may happen gradually. But over and over again, we can look back at situations we have walked through and see how God worked them out as we leaned on the supernatural help of the Holy Spirit.

This is especially important to realize when praying for other people. God hears our prayers for them, but He is having to work with their will or with what they want. He also is working with the right timing in their lives and with situations we are not aware of. Therefore, the "answer" to our prayers may not be what we envisioned when we prayed. When we pray for people and God works things out for their *good*, we can be just as grateful as when He answers the rest of our prayers, even if the answer is not what we were expecting.

One of the ongoing blessings of praying in our prayer language is the supernatural help of the Holy Spirit in causing everything to work together for good.

The Holy Spirit is our Great Helper in prayer!

Reflection Questions

1. Can you think of a time when someone prayed for you in the Spirit?

2. Do you know of anyone who needs the Holy Spirit's conviction concerning their relationship with God? How could they benefit from prayer in the Spirit?

3. Has God ever worked something out for you in answer to your prayer that was not the way you envisioned it would work out? Did it happen gradually? As you ponder this, can you see how God actually worked it out for good?

CHAPTER 7

WATCHING IN THE SPIRIT

Praying always with all prayer and supplication <u>in the Spirit, and watching thereunto</u> with all perseverance and supplication for all saints ...
Ephesians 6:18 KJV, emphasis added

To be on watch in military terms means to carefully look and listen for any warning signs of danger or coming attack. Similarly, the Bible teaches us that we are to be on watch spiritually. God's Word instructs us to be alert and watch against temptation (see Mark 14:38; 1 Peter 5:8). We are also told to watch and be alert when in prayer (see Colossians 4:2). And the opening scripture shows us that now, by using our prayer language, we can *watch in the Spirit.*

Watching in the Spirit is another great benefit of praying in our prayer language. When we pray in our prayer language, we pray about things that haven't happened yet but will happen today, tomorrow, and in the future. That's because the Spirit—who knows God's thoughts—is praying and not we ourselves. God knows tomorrow; He knows what is waiting in our future.

God also knows what our spiritual enemy has planned for us. Jesus once told Peter (also called Simon) that Satan had plans to "sift him as wheat":

Simon, Simon, Satan has asked to sift all of you as wheat. But I have prayed for you, Simon, that your faith may not fail. And when you have turned back, strengthen your brothers. (Luke 22:31–32 NIV)

Jesus knew that Satan had plans for Peter, but He told Peter that He had prayed for him and that Satan's plans for Peter and the disciples would not be fulfilled.

God also knows what He has planned for us:

For we are God's [own] handiwork (His workmanship), recreated in Christ Jesus, [born anew] that we may do those good works which God predestined (planned beforehand) for us [taking paths which He prepared ahead of time], that we should walk in them [living the good life which He prearranged and made ready for us to live]. (Ephesians 2:10 AMPC, emphasis added)

Our spiritual enemy has evil plans for us, and our Heavenly Father has good plans for us. So we are told to *watch*. We can diligently strive to apply the truths of God's Word to our lives, being alert against temptation. We can bring our requests to Him—our needs and the needs of others. These are ways we watch and pray in our daily lives.

But now that we are filled with the Spirit, we can also watch in the Spirit. One of the great features of the Holy Spirit's help in prayer is His ability to *go ahead* in the spiritual realm. So when we pray in our prayer language, we go ahead of our day and go ahead of any evil planned against us. Essentially, we are giving the Holy Spirit an opportunity to go into our future and pray.

This is important because although God has plans for our lives and Christ has defeated our spiritual enemy, we still live on earth where two kingdoms are operating: the kingdom of darkness and the Kingdom of light. But we have confidence because the Word teaches that we are no longer under the enemy's rule. *"For he has rescued us from the kingdom of darkness and transferred us into the Kingdom of his dear Son, who purchased our freedom and forgave our sins"* (Colossians 1:13–14 NLT).

When we are praying in the Spirit, we pray *through* the darkness of the enemy's kingdom (his evil plans and desires for us) *to* the place of victory (God's good plans and desires for us).

We all know what it is like to pray *after* evil has touched our lives. Watching in the Spirit enables us to pray *before* the evil happens.

Does the advantage of praying in the Spirit sound too good to be true? To our minds it may seem like an impossibility, but it is a reality when we pray with the help of the Holy Spirit.

God can do much with our prayers in the Spirit. Many evil plans can be stopped, allowing God's plans to go forth. Then we can walk out in our daily lives what we have been praying through in our prayer lives—freedom, answered prayers, and victories on the paths that God has prepared for us!

Reflection Questions

1. How can watching in the Spirit keep us spiritually, physically, and mentally safe?

2. Do you believe that God has good plans and desires for your life? In what areas of your life have you seen His goodness?

3. Have you ever experienced evil plans being stopped because of prayer?

CHAPTER 8

RECEIVING COMFORT FROM THE SPIRIT

And I will pray the Father, and he shall give you another
<u>Comforter</u>, that he may abide with you for ever ...
John 14:16 KJV, emphasis added

We are discovering the ways praying in our prayer language enhances our lives. God answers these prayers in many ways, sometimes by simply working things out for us as we saw in Chapter 6 (p. 31). But there is one benefit that we receive with every prayer in the Spirit. The immediate and present benefit of this praying is *comfort*.

Some translations of John 14:16 call the Holy Spirit our *Comforter*. Comfort is one of the blessings we receive when we pray in our prayer language. This comfort is especially needed when we are facing trials in our lives.

I have a video from the day my oldest daughter was born. Several family members had arrived at the birth center to see the new baby. When she was less than an hour old, the midwife had to disrupt her sleep to weigh her. My five-year-old niece and my cousin looked on in concern as the newborn screamed at the top of her little lungs. But the midwife calmly and quietly said to the girls, "Watch what happens when I wrap her back up in her blanket." She then tightly swaddled the baby in the blanket, and within seconds the baby quieted down. The girls, now relieved, ran off to play.

How could the midwife be so confident that the baby would stop crying immediately after being wrapped up in her blanket? She knew because she had seen it happen time and time again. A baby cries like it's the end of the world, but wrapping the baby tightly in a soft blanket makes it feel warm and secure.

I can confidently tell you that the Holy Spirit will bring you comfort when you pray in your prayer language. Your circumstances may make you feel like it's the end of the world, and you may feel like crying at the top of your lungs. But no matter what the situation is, He will bring comfort to you every time you pray. *Every single time.*

I constantly experience this comfort in prayer. It works like this: I may be dealing with a difficult situation, so I share my problem with my loving Heavenly Father and then start to pray in my prayer language. Before long, He begins to comfort me. I may not have remembered to tell God all the details, but I am feeling better. My mind hasn't even figured how my problem is going to work out yet, but I have peace. The circumstance hasn't changed, but I feel hope rising in me.

In the crises of life, it is important to remember that while you pray in the Spirit you are praying the will of God for your situation. You can be sure He is working on your behalf. But as your good and loving Heavenly Father, He's also bringing you the *present comfort* you need. When you begin to experience His comfort, receive it by trusting Him and resting in His comfort as a newborn baby rests in a soft blanket.

But you will need to take His comfort a step further. The difference between you and a newborn is that you can't stay in that "blanket" all day! You must go back into the natural world and face those circumstances you just prayed about in the Spirit. His comfort is for your *strength*. So take some time to remind yourself of His Word about your situation, which will provide you with an assurance of victory as you leave your time of prayer.

Praying in our prayer language brings comfort from the Holy Spirit, our Comforter.

Reflection Questions

1. How does the fact that Jesus called the Holy Spirit our Comforter make you feel?

2. Have you ever experienced the comfort of the Holy Spirit?

3. Could knowing that the Holy Spirit is your Comforter be a motivation for you to pray in your prayer language the next time you find yourself in a difficult situation?

CHAPTER 9

ENJOYING THE RIVERS

... rivers of living water will flow out from their heart.
John 7:38 ERV

My husband was a youth pastor for several years. Every summer, we would take the teenagers river tubing. We would spend the day relaxing on inner tubes while the river's current just carried us along. If the kids wanted to stay with their friends, they had to hold on to each other's tubes or the river would carry them away. When it was time to get out, we had to quickly grab on to a tree limb and step out on the rocks while the river kept flowing past us. The river was flowing when we arrived, and the river was flowing when we left.

In this chapter, I would like to share with you the great blessing the Holy Spirit is in our time with God, as Jesus describes in the following passage:

The last day of the festival came. It was the most important day. On that day Jesus stood up and said loudly, "Whoever is thirsty may come to me and drink. If anyone believes in me, <u>rivers of living water will flow out from their heart</u>. That is what the Scriptures say." <u>Jesus was talking about the Spirit</u>. The Spirit had not yet been given to people, because Jesus had not yet been raised to glory. But later, those who believed in Jesus would receive the Spirit. (John 7:37–39 ERV, emphasis added).

As we begin to pray in our prayer language, we step into these rivers of living water. And once we step in, prayer becomes just as easy and as natural as floating in a river.

Spending time praying in the Spirit is one of the biggest spiritual favors you can do for yourself. Why? Because as you charge up your spirit as we discussed in Chapter 2 (p. 7), you step into a river of the Spirit, and you step into a "want to."

Once we are in the river of prayer we *want to* stay in the river. There is something so comforting and peaceful about the Holy Spirit. Now that we are here we want to continue to be with Him. The Holy Spirit puts the "want to" in praying for the situations in our lives that need our attention. He puts the "want to" into studying God's Word. He puts the "want to" into worshiping Him. He puts the "want to" into meditating on God's promises. He puts the "want to" into being quiet in His presence. He even puts the "want to" into receiving His gentle correction.

It is wonderful when our time with God is not out of duty and obligation. We are not just praying because we know we *should* pray. Taking time out to spend with God does require discipline and diligence. We will probably have to break away from some other things to spend time with Him. But disciplining ourselves to take time to pray in the Spirit is so worth our while because once we are actually praying, the river will carry us, making prayer so much more enjoyable than praying without His help.

And because these rivers of prayer never stop flowing, don't be surprised if you won't *want* to leave your time with God. You'll be enjoying the "living water" flowing out of your own heart, bringing life, joy, peace, and comfort from God.

If this is the kind of relationship with God you're longing for, the rivers are waiting to carry you there as you begin to pray in your prayer language.

Reflection Questions

1. Do you struggle with disciplining yourself to spend time with God?

2. How could a "want to" change your view of prayer?

3. Have you experienced moments with God so wonderful that you do not want to leave your time with Him?

CHAPTER 10

ARRIVING AT VICTORY

I will sing with my spirit.
1 Corinthians 14:15 ERV

Most of us have busy schedules and only have so much time to pray before we must go about the business of the day. Praying in our prayer language can be a wonderful blessing to this daily time with God. But how much time should we give to praying in the Spirit? Since our mind doesn't know what we are saying in this language, how will we know when our prayer is finished?

Let's say we board a train that runs from Virginia to Florida, departing Virginia in the evening and arriving in Florida the next morning. Much of the ride is spent traveling in the dark. Looking out the window, there's not much to see in the darkness except land and trees. So we sit back, relax, read a book, or take a nap. Eventually, in the early hours of the morning, we begin to see signs that we are approaching our destination. The sun begins to rise, and we see palm trees emerging in the light—a sure sign that we are nearing Florida. Before long, the train begins to slow down as it enters the terminal. We gather our belongings and exit the train, ready to enjoy our destination.

That's how a train trip usually goes. But what if during our travel in the middle of the night, we started to have some questions. "It's so dark outside. How do I know if the train is really going to Florida?" "What if I'm just wasting my time?" "Does the conductor really know how to get me there?" And then what if all those doubts and fears make you think, "I should just jump off the train and find another way to get there." That would be ridiculous! Of course, we don't have these questions during a train ride. We just trust that the train is taking us to our destination.

In the same way, much of the time praying in the Spirit is "in the dark." Our minds can begin to question if we are accomplishing anything. We think, "Maybe I'm wasting my time when I could be doing something else." But when thoughts like that begin to fill our minds, we must continue to "ride" on this prayer and not "jump off the train." Remember, we are charging our spirits, praying the will of God, and speaking mysteries while the Holy Spirit searches the deep treasures of victory God has planned for us (see Chapters 2–5, pp. 7–30).

Before long, signs that we are nearing our destination will begin to appear. Our spirits begin to feel lighter and at peace. The things that were bothering us when we began to pray have become less of a burden. Our faith is strengthened. When we experience one of those signs—no matter how small it is—we can be assured that the Holy Spirit has accomplished what He wanted to in prayer. The Holy Spirit is letting us know that whatever we needed to say to God has been said, and now we can give God praise!

Just like we praise God in our normal language after we have prayed from our minds, our spirits can begin to praise God in our prayer language. But the difference is we will be praising and glorifying God with the supernatural help of the Holy Spirit.

We can choose at this point to sing with our spirit by letting a little song of praise come up in our prayer language. Victory is a *destination* in the Spirit. Singing in the Spirit is enjoying that destination!

If I pray in a different language, my spirit is praying, but my mind does nothing. So what should I do? I will pray with my spirit, but I will also pray with my mind. <u>I will sing with my spirit</u>, but I will also sing with my mind. (1 Corinthians 14:14–15 ERV, emphasis added)

We see in these verses that praying in the Spirit is a decision we make: *"I will pray with my spirit."* And we also see that singing in the Spirit is a decision we make: *"I will sing with my spirit."* Singing in the Spirit is as equally supernatural as praying in the Spirit. There is a purpose for it, just like there is a purpose for our praying. Although our minds do not understand what we are singing, we are thanking God "in a good way!" (see 1 Corinthians 14:17 ERV, punctuation added).

I have experienced this victory many times at the end of my prayer time. Did my circumstances change? No, at least not in the natural realm. But something did change. The concern I felt for the circumstances I was walking through turned into peace and assurance that all would be well. There are people who would give all the money they have to experience this kind of peace and assurance. That's why it's important for us to see that God has provided these blessings through the means of praying in our prayer language.

God knows you have a busy life. He will help you reach your destination of victory in the time you have set aside to pray. Your mind will not understand how this happens because it is not mental prayer; it is Spirit-empowered prayer that God designed to help us triumph in life.

You will be amazed at how riding the prayer train in the Spirit will take you to a destination of victory!

Reflection Questions

1. When you pray in the Spirit, what thoughts cross your mind that tempt you to stop praying? What specific scriptures will you use to cancel those thoughts and keep praying?

2. Have you ever sung in the Spirit before? If not, is this something that you will decide to try?

3. Praying in the Spirit can feel like being "in the dark," but we can continue to pray until we start to see signs of victory. What specific actions will you take to ensure that you keep riding the prayer train and don't jump off?

CHAPTER 11

STAYING FULL OF THE SPIRIT

... be filled with the Spirit ...
Ephesians 5:18 GW

We have looked at many ways our prayer life is blessed when we receive the baptism of the Holy Spirit and begin to pray in our new prayer language. If only we could stay in that place of prayer all day! It would be wonderful to have the same feeling throughout our day as we did when we ended our time with God. Well, He has provided a way for us to be full of the Spirit throughout our busy day.

Don't get drunk on wine, which leads to wild living. Instead, be filled with the Spirit by reciting psalms, hymns, and spiritual songs for your own good. Sing and make music to the Lord with your hearts. (Ephesians 5:18–19 GW)

This scripture tells us we can *"be filled with the Spirit"* even after we leave our time of prayer.

In the previous chapters, I discussed praying in our prayer language. In this chapter, I would like to show you how you can be continually filled with the Spirit, not by praying in your prayer language, but by speaking to God from your heart in your normal language.

We are filled with the Spirit by reciting (some translations say, "speaking to yourselves in") "psalms, hymns, and spiritual songs." Merriam-Webster's dictionary describes a *psalm* as "a sacred song or poem used in worship" and a *hymn* as "a song of praise to God." A spiritual song, one of worship, does not have to be one that we have heard before, such as a worship song we sing at church. A spiritual song can be one that we make up as the Ephesians 5 verse says, *"sing and <u>make</u> music to the Lord"* (emphasis added).

Reciting, speaking, and singing about the Lord and to the Lord may seem like a great challenge in the busyness of our daily lives. But God knows that we are busy and have a lot on our minds every day, so He provided a way for us to keep connecting with Him all day—with and in our *hearts*.

You see, our hearts can continue to talk to the Lord, sing to Him, and worship Him even in the midst of having many things on our minds and many daily activities on our plates. Our hearts can recite hymns, poems, and songs that our hearts have made up to Him while our minds and bodies are busy doing other things.

This ongoing worship is kind of like the background music we hear in public places, like at doctors' offices and restaurants. We hear the music playing, but it does not stop us from doing the business or activity we are there to do. Someone turns the music on, and it plays continually in the background.

We can simply *turn on* worship to God at the beginning of our day. And then we can speak and sing to the Lord from our hearts throughout the rest of the day, even while other things are going on around us. When we have a minute between our busy activities, we can begin to worship God. If we are alone, we can worship Him out loud from our heart. If people are around, we can worship Him quietly in our heart. Building these simple acts of worship into our lives is how we can stay filled with the Spirit throughout the day, every day.

Even after we leave our time of Spirit-empowered prayer, we can continue to stay full of the Spirit!

Reflection Questions

1. Do you find it hard to keep your fellowship with God going after your prayer time ends? How can you continue to be filled with the Spirit throughout the day?

2. Could you take a few minutes every day to begin a song in your heart to the Lord?

3. Our focus scripture teaches how to be filled with the Spirit *"for your own good"* (emphasis added). How do you think staying full of the Spirit would affect your daily life?

ADDITIONAL RESOURCES

For further study on Spirit-empowered prayer, you can consult the following resources. The list starts with foundational books on this topic and builds to more in-depth ones.

- *The Holy Spirit Today,* by John Siebeling
  (Distributed by Amazon and The Life Church, 2009)

- *Getting a Grip on the Spirit-Empowered Life: Stepping into a Deeper Experience with the Holy Spirit,* by Beth Jones
  (Published by Harrison House, 2019)

- *The God I Never Knew: How Real Friendship with the Holy Spirit Can Change Your Life,* by Robert Morris
  (Published by Random House, 2011)

- *The Beauty of Spiritual Language: Unveiling the Mystery of Speaking in Tongues,* by Jack Hayford
  (Published by Gateway, 2018)

- *The Master Is Calling: Discovering the Wonders of Spirit-Led Prayer,* by Lynne Hammond
  (Published by Whitaker House, 2000)

- *Tongues: Beyond the Upper Room,* by Kenneth E. Hagin
  (Published by RHEMA Bible Church, 2007)

ABOUT THE AUTHOR

Stephanie Trayers and her husband, Eddie Trayers, are the lead pastors of Summit Church, a thriving multicultural congregation in the Washington, D.C., metropolitan area. Stephanie is an avid teacher, sharing with the Summit community the basics that bring everyday sustaining power for the follower of Jesus Christ. She demonstrates a lifestyle of connection to God through her example of a life of prayer, and she makes a purposeful impact in the lives of the people of Summit Church. She enjoys reading, baking, and spending time in the mountains of Virginia. Eddie and Stephanie have been married for more than 30 years, and they have two grown daughters, Tori and Megan.